Cross Cultural Idioms and Expressions

By Vladimir Marshak

Contents

The main idea of this book

Languages are my passion. I studied English for many years, step by step: vocabulary, grammar etc. From my point of view, the idioms and sayings are the most interesting and difficult part of every language.

I have read many books of idioms, proverbs and sayings, and in almost every book there were common idioms and those that even educated native speakers did not know.

I'm a native Russian speaker with Hebrew bilingual proficiency and a good command of English. I came to the interesting conclusion that if we have the same idiom in English Russian and Hebrew, it is the litmus test that confirms the idiom is very common and useful in every language.

In my book there are English, Russian and Hebrew idioms and sayings that have exactly the same meanings in English, Russian and Hebrew (but not always the same translation).

For example:

Call a spade a spade

לקרוא ילד בשמו (Literal meaning: to call the child by their name)

Называть вещи своими именами (Literal meaning: to call the things by their names)

This idiom has the exact same meaning in English, Russian and Hebrew: to say exactly what you think in a straightforward and maybe blunt manner about unpleasant things.

Who is this book for?

If you are interested in English, Russian or Hebrew, and would like to know quite common and useful idioms, proverbs and sayings in these languages, then this book is for you.

Key

The English, Hebrew and Russian idioms in this book have the same meaning, but not always the same literal meaning. When a Hebrew or Russian idiom has the same literal meaning as the English idiom it is followed by the sign <>.

When Hebrew or Russian idioms have different literal meanings than the English idiom it is followed by the literal translation to English in parentheses.

Idioms and sayings from A to Z

A

Achilles' heel

עקב אכילס<>

Ахиллесова пята <>

Meaning: A weak point of a strong person. The term "Achilles' heel" refers to the mythological hero Achilles, whose only weak point was a spot on his heel.

Example: Sarah is a brilliant student but math is her Achilles' heel.

Actions speak louder than words

מעשים חזקים ממילים (Actions are stronger than words)

Дела важнее слов (Actions are more important than words)

Meaning: A person may say one thing, but how they act reveals their true feelings and character.

Example: Molly always invites me over, but when I show up she says she is too busy to see me. I guess her actions speak louder than words.

A bird in the hand is worth two in the bush

טוב ציפור אחד ביד משתיים על העץ<>

Лучше синица в руках, чем журавль в небе (Better a tit in the hands than a crane in the sky)

Meaning: You should value what you already possess, and not wish for something you may never have, even if it seems better.

Example: John has a very demanding and difficult job. But given the unstable job market, he does not want to quit until he finds a better one. A bird in the hand is worth two in the bush!

A blessing in disguise

ברכה בתחפושת<>

Нет худа без добра (No bad without good)

Meaning: Something that does not seem good or positive, but turns out to be helpful.

Example: The tree that fell on our garage turned out to be a blessing in disguise. The insurance company gave us money to fix it, and it turned out to be enough to build a larger one!

A figment of the imagination

פרי הדמיון (Fruit of the imagination)

Плод воображения (Fruit of the imagination)

Meaning: Something that is not real, imagined by a person.

Example: My little niece Louisa says she has a purple kitten, but it is a just a figment of her imagination.

A land of milk and honey

<>ארץ זבת חלב ודבש

Страна текущая молоком и мёдом <>

Meaning: This is a biblical reference to Israel. This idiom means that a certain place is beautiful and overflowing with wonderful things.

Example: When the seamstress walked into the silk warehouse, it was as if she were in the land of milk and honey.

A little bird told me

ציפור קטנה לחשה לי (A little bird whispered to me)

Слухами земля полнится (A land is full of gossip)

Meaning: This idiom indicates in a nice way that somebody does not want to reveal the source of their information.

Example: "Mary, I heard you are expecting!"

"What? How did you find out?"

"Oh, a little bird told me."

A matter of life and death

שאלה של חיים ומוות (Question of life and death)

Вопрос жизни и смерти (Question of life and death)

Meaning: This means that something is extremely important and will have severe consequences and impacts on lives.

Example: Kimberly knew that getting the money for the operation was a matter of life and death.

A lot of water has passed under the bridge

מים רבים זרמו בנהר   (A lot of water passed in the river)

Много воды утекло (A lot of water passed)

Meaning: Enough time has passed for things to be forgiven or forgotten.

Example: Tom didn't mind seeing his old college rival, since a lot of water has passed under the bridge.

Add fuel to the fire

<<להוסיף שמן למדורה

Лить масло в огонь<>

Meaning: To add more stress or problems to an already difficult situation.

Example: John was about to bring up what happened at the last business dinner, but his boss begged him not to add fuel to the fire.

Add insult to injury

לזרות מלך על הפצעים (Putting salt on a wound)

Сыпать соль на раны (Putting salt on a wound)

Meaning: To heap another offense onto an already offended person or troubled situation.

Example: John came late to the meeting and then, adding insult to injury, he failed in his presentation.

Afraid of your own shadow

<>לפחד מהצל של עצמך

Бояться собственной тени <>

Meaning: To be extremely fearful, usually without good reason.

Example: I wouldn't put her in charge of security at the meeting because she's afraid of her own shadow.

Ahead of one's time

לפני זמנו (Before his time)

Впереди своего времени <>

Meaning: Particularly bright or mature, unexpectedly brilliant, but in a way people cannot relate to or do not understand.

Example: Many people did not like Mozart's music when he was alive. Now he is considered a musical genius, so perhaps he was ahead of his time.

All for one and one for all

<>כולם בשביל אחד ואחד בשביל כולם

Один за всех и все за одного<>

Meaning: All members of a group are equally devoted to each other.

Example: The motto of the basketball team is all for one and one for all. You have never seen a better or more united team, so it must be a great motto for them.

All that glitters is not gold

<>לא כל הנוצץ זהב

Не всё золото что блестит<>

Meaning: Appearances can be deceptive.

Example: Stephanie thought taking the promotion would be great, but she didn't realize how many more hours she had to put in. Now she realizes all that glitters is not gold.

All your eggs in one basket

<>כל הביצים בסל אחד

Все яйца в одной корзине <>

Meaning: To be dependent on one thing or one person, or to invest money in only one project without any backup plan.

Example: I told Nelson not to invest all of his money in one stock, but he didn't listen. I hope he won't regret putting all his eggs in one basket.

All good things come to an end

<>כל הדברים הטובים מגיעים לקיצם

Всё хорошее когда нибудь заканчивается(All good some time ends)

Meaning: Everything, even the best things, have to conclude eventually.

Example: We had a blast at the amusement park, but now it is time to go home. All good things must come to an end.

All's well that ends well

<>הכול טוב מה שנגמר בטוב

Всё хорошо, что хорошо кончается<>

Meaning: As long as something ends in a satisfactory manner, it doesn't matter what went wrong earlier in the process.

Example: It was a rough day driving in bad weather, but we arrived at our destination safely. All's well that ends well.

Appetite comes with eating

עם האוכל בא התיאבון<>

Аппетит приходит во время еды<>

Meaning: As you begin something, your desire to continue it grows.

Example: Getting into the habit of jogging was hard at first, but I just finished my first marathon. I guess in regards to my exercise habits, appetite comes with eating.

Apple doesn't fall far from the tree

התפוח לא נופל רחוק מהעץ<>

Яблоко от яблони не далеко падает <>

Meaning: Children will often act like their parents, and do not distance themselves from the things they learned from watching how their parents act.

Example: I heard that Coach Smith's son got a job as an assistant coach at another school. I guess the apple didn't fall from the tree in their family!

far

Armed to the teeth

חמוש מכף הרגל(Armed from the foot)

Вооружен до зубов<>

Meaning: Well-equipped and prepared.

Example: I knew Jason's mother was mad about what happened, but I didn't expect her to show up armed to the teeth!

Asleep at the switch

להרדם בשמירה(Asleep at guarding)

Заснуть за штурвалом<>

Meaning: Neglecting your job, duties, or responsibilities.

Example: The Sharks just scored another goal! I guess the goalie of the visiting team must be asleep at the switch today!

At the end of the day

<>בסופו של יום

В конце концов (finally)

Meaning: At the end of a situation, in conclusion.

Example: Well, at the end of the day, the parties came to an agreement, and now the merger is moving forward.

Automatic pilot

<>טייס אוטומטי

Автопилот <>

Meaning: Acting instinctively and reflexively, not acting with plans and careful thoughts.

Example: John did not pay attention on what happened around him; he was on automatic pilot.

B

Ball in your court

<>הכדור במגרש שלך

Мяч на твоём поле <>

Meaning: The matter now rests in your hands; it is up to you to say the next thing, or take the next action.

Example: I have called Harrison three times, and I refuse to call again. The ball is in his court.

Banana republic

<>רפובליקת בננות

Банановая республика<>

Meaning: Small dependent country ruling by a corrupt dictator.

Example: With all the bickering, the town council meeting gave the impression of a banana republic instead of one of the top ten cities in the country.

Barking dogs seldom bite

כלב נובח אינו נושך(Barking dogs do not bite)

Собака, что лает — редко кусает<>

Meaning: People may make a lot of aggressive statements, often without intending to back up their threats.

Example: John speaks aggressively, but never causes any damage. Barking dogs seldom bite.

Bark up the wrong tree

לנבוח על העץ הלא נכון<>

Напасть на ложный след (Attack the wrong track)

Meaning: You have the wrong idea, or are confused.

Example: Phoebe was barking up the wrong tree when she accused Matthew of stealing her ring.

Beat around the bush

ללכת סחור וסחור(Go round and round)

Ходить вокруг да около (Go around and near)

Meaning: Speaking a lot instead of going straight to the point.

Example: Stop beating around the bush and ask me exactly what you want.

Beauty is in the eye of the beholder

<>היופי הוא בעיני המתבונן

Красота в глазах смотрящего (Beauty is in the eye of the observer)

Meaning: Everyone has a different standard of beauty.

Example: Beauty is in the eye of the beholder when it comes to art. I can't stand modern art, but my sister loves it.

Behind the scenes

<>מאחורי הקלעים

За кулисами <>

Meaning: There is an action that occurs that isn't seen/shown behind the main events.

Example: The principal took credit for the school fundraiser, but everyone knew that his secretary did all the behind-the-scenes work to make it a success.

Be in someone else's shoes

<>להיות בנעליים של מישהו אחר

Оказаться на чужом месте (To be in place of somebody)

Meaning: To understand another person's point of view or experience.

Example: Timmy complained about his own chores, but when he traded chores with his sister for the week and spent time in her shoes, he realized he had it easy.

Be between life and death

<<>להיות בין החיים למוות

Быть между жизнью и смертью <>

Meaning: When a person has an equal chance of living or dying.

Example: Jed's surgery is risky. If he makes it out of recovery, he'll be between life and death for several days.

Be in the spotlight

להיות באור הזקורים (Be in the limelight)

Быть в центре внимания (To be in the center of attention)

Meaning: To be the center of attention.

Example: Angela was quick to volunteer to lead the expedition, as she loves to be in the spotlight.

Below the belt

מתתחת לחגורה<>

Ниже пояса <>

Meaning: To hit below the belt is an illegal move in boxing, indicating underhand, injurious behavior.

Example: I know Ron and Poppy are in a custody battle, but to show compromising photos from twenty years ago was really hitting below the belt.

Bend over backward

לעשות שמיניות באוויר (To make figure-eights in the air)

Прыгнуть выше головы (Jump over the head)

Meaning: To do everything possible, even to the extreme, to accommodate, appease, or help someone.

Example: Loren is bending over backward to make sure his first hotel guests are happy.

Better late than never

<>מוטב מאוחר מלעולם לא

Лучше поздно чем никогда<>

Meaning: It is better to have something, even if it was not completed on time, or after the fact.

Example: I finally got a gift from my cousin for the birth of my son. My son is almost a year old now, but better late than never.

Better than nothing

<>יותר טוב מכלום

Лучше, чем ничего<>

Meaning: Better to receive something even if it is of poor or inadequate quality than nothing.

Example: The thin coat didn't do much to keep out the heavy snow, but it was better than nothing.

Between a rock and a hard place

<בין הפטיש לסדן<>

Между молотом и наковальней (Between the upper and the nether millstone)

Meaning: Being put a position of having two very difficult options as your only choices.

Example: Horace could go through the dark, dangerous tunnel, or across the alligator-infested river. He was between a rock and a hard place.

Bitter pill to swallow

<גלולה מרה לבלוע<>

Проглотить горькую пилюлю <>

Meaning: It is a very sad or difficult thing to accept.

Example: Joan finally realized that her sister would not fight her cocaine addiction, but it was a very bitter pill to swallow.

Bite the hand that feeds you

<<לנשוך את היד המאכילה אותך

Кусать руку, которая тебя кормит<>

Meaning: To treat someone who has helped you in a mean and ungrateful manner.

Example: Terrance really bit the hand that feeds him when he refused to help his manager yesterday.

Blank check

<<שיק פתוח

Карт-бланш (Carte blanche)

Meaning: Having freedom to do whatever you need or want to do, usually in the context of a project.

Example: Finish the new wing of the museum however you want, the curator gave us a blank check on it.

Bite the tongue

<לנשוך את הלשון>

Прикусить язык<>

Meaning: To stop speaking, usually given as a warning or admonishment.

Example: Before Maurice could say one more word, his mother hissed, "Bite your tongue!"

Blue blood

<דם כחול>

Голубая кровь <>

Meaning: Someone having, or behaving as if they have, royal and aristocratic heritage.

Example: The Du Val family claims to be old Kentucky blue bloods, but we know they are simply pretentious.

Born yesterday

<>נולד אתמול

Лыком шиты (Basted sloppily)

Meaning: To be born yesterday means that a person is very innocent or naive.

Example: "I wasn't born yesterday! Don't expect me to believe your lies," Alex warned his girlfriend.

Born with a silver spoon in one's mouth

<>נולד עם כפית של זהב בפה

Родился в рубашке (Born in a shirt)

Meaning: To be born into a family with wealth or power.

Example: No one expected Janine to get a job after college. After all, she was born with a silver spoon in her mouth and had plenty of money in her trust fund.

Bread and circuses

לחם ושעשועים (Bread and entertainment)

Хлеба и зрелищ (Bread and entertainment)

Meaning: How people in power appease the disgruntled public, with food and spectacle or entertainment.

Example: If the newly elected president thinks winning people over will be a matter of bread and circuses, he will be in for a shock.

Build castles in the air

<>לבנות מגדלים באוויר

Строить воздушные замки<>

Meaning: Having fantastical ideas and whims that are unrealistic.

Example: I wish Julian would focus on completing his degree instead of building castles in the air.

Bull in a china shop

פיל בחנות חרסינה (Elephant in a china shop)

Слон в посудной лавке (Elephant in a china shop)

Meaning: Someone who is extremely out of place, and possibly destructive.

Example: This politician is not diplomatic; he behaves like a bull in a china shop.

Burn bridges

<>לשרוף גשרים

Сжигать мосты <>

Meaning: To completely and finally cut ties and break off relationships with someone.

Example: Sal was so angry when she quit her job, that she burnt all the bridges she had with that company.

Bury the head in the sand

<>לטמון ראש בחול

Спрятать голову в песок <>

Meaning: To ignore the situation (particularly a bad one) that is happening around you.

Example: Kimmy buried her head in the sand and refused to acknowledge all the evidence that her husband was having an affair.

Butterflies in the stomach

<>פרפרים בבטן

На душе кошки скребут (Cats scratch your soul)

Meaning: To feel very excited or nervous, as if something is fluttering inside.

Example: As Sasha waited for the curtain to rise, she felt the butterflies in her stomach start to fade.

Buy time

להרוויח את הזמן (Win time)

Выиграть время (Win time)

Meaning: To postpone an event with the aim of allowing a better alternative to present itself.

Example: John bought time by claiming he was sick in order to study for the test.

C

Call a spade a spade

לקרוא לילד בשמו (To name a child by his name)

Называть вещи своими именами (To name the things by their names)

Meaning: Bluntly state the facts without trying to be nice.

Example: Let's call a spade a spade and admit Uncle Herbert is too old to drive at night.

Calm before the storm

<>השקט לפני הסערה

Затишье перед бурей<>

Meaning: A lull or period of inaction before hectic/unpleasant events start.

Example: Rhonda knew her six boys would be home from school in an hour, so she decided to enjoy the calm before the storm with a good book.

Can't see the forest for the trees

<>מרוב עצים לא יראה היער

Не видит леса за деревьями <>

Meaning: To be unaware of something that is plainly right in front of you, often referring to concentrating on a small issue while the larger issue is ignored.

Example: Alan is so obsessed with completing his car collection that he is oblivious to the strain it puts on his finances. It is one of those situations where he can't see the forest for the trees.

Cards on the table

<>קלפים על השולחן

Открыть карты (Open the cards)

Meaning: To give all your information to someone as honestly as possible.

Example: I have to lay my cards on the table and admit that I can't go through with the deal without more money.

Caught red handed

לתפוס על החם (To catch somebody on hot)

На воре шапка горит (A thief's cap is on fire)

Meaning: To be caught in the act of committing a crime or some offense, or just to be caught doing something unexpectedly.

Example: Uri caught Samantha red-handed as she left a secret-admirer note at his desk.

Carrot and stick

<>מקל וגזר

Кнут и пряник (Whip and cake)

Meaning: Using a motivator and a threat in order to compel somebody to do something.

Example: High classes usually use a carrot and stick to subjugate low classes.

Character assassination

<>רצח אופי

Злобная клевета (malicious slander)

Meaning: To slander and destroy someone's reputation with false claims.

Example: It was pure character assassination when Whitney claimed that Brenda was running a brothel from her house.

Chicken-and-egg

<>ביצה ותרנגול

Курица или яйцо<>

Meaning: A debate about the order of events, as in, which came first: did the chicken lay the egg, or did the egg hatch and out came the chicken?

Example: I wish the girls would stop their chicken-and-egg argument over who Brad liked first.

Choose the lesser of two evils

<>לבחור את הרע במיעוטו

Выбрать меньшее из двух зол <>

Meaning: When given two bad options, try to pick the one that will do the least harm.

Example: I don't like either of the candidates, but I'll try to choose the lesser of two evils.

Clear as a bell

פשוט כשמש (Simple as the sun)

Ясно как божий день (It is clear as day)

Meaning: To hear something or understand something with complete clarity.

Example: I never understood geometry before, but when Mrs. Wells taught me it was as clear as a bell.

Cold comfort

נחמה פורתא (Small comfort)

Слабое утешение (Weak comfort)

Meaning: Something may provide relief, but it is not actually providing the happiness and peace one usually associates with comfort.

Example: After losing the big project, finding a small client was cold comfort.

Come out of the closet

<>לצאת מהארון

Выйти из тени, публично заявить (Come out of the shadow, publicly claim)

Meaning: To reveal a person's true nature, or a guarded secret. It is usually referenced when talking about revealing sexual orientation.

Example: Bethany came out of the closet and introduced her girlfriend to her parents.

Come what may

יהיה מה שיהיה(What will be will be)

Будь что будет (What will be will be)

Meaning: Whatever occurs, a person will see their aim to do something through to the end.

Example: We are going to proceed with the mountaineering expedition, come what may.

Common denominator

<>מכנה משותף

Общий знаменатель <>

Meaning: The common or similar basis that two items or people share.

Example: Joy and Elsa are very different, but they share the common denominator of being new to the company.

Compare apples and oranges

<>להשוות תפוזים לתפוחים

Сравнивать яблоки с апельсинами<>

Meaning: Refers to warning people not to compare two dissimilar objects, the idea being that it is not a fair or accurate comparison.

Example: You can't compare Mr. McGonal, a veteran pilot, to the new rookie out of flight school. That's like comparing apples to oranges.

Cream of the crop

דובדבן שבקצפת (Cherry in whipped cream)

Сливки в шоколаде (Cream in chocolate)

Meaning: The very best that someone has to offer.

Example: Cartier's is the cream of the crop in the jewelry world

Crocodile tears

דמעות של תנין<>

Крокодиловы слёзы <>

Meaning: Expressing fake sadness or sorrow that is insincere.

Example: John's young second wife inherited millions after his death. His children suspected her grief was all crocodile tears.

Cross the Rubicon

לחצות את הרוביקון<>

Перейти Рубикон <>

Meaning: Taking serious irreversible action.

Example: He crossed the Rubicon when he sent the letter with the severe accusations.

Cut corners

לעגל פינות(Round the corners)

Срезать острые углы (Cut sharp corners)

Meaning: Taking shortcuts or completing work in a shoddy or cheap way that impacts the quality.

Example: Tell the wedding planner not to cut any corners; everything must be perfect for my daughter's special day.

D

Deep pockets

<>כיס עמוק

Глубокие карманы <>

Meaning: Having a lot of wealth and money.

Example: Mr. Koning has deep pockets; it is nothing for him to buy a new car every year.

Die of boredom

<>מתים משעמום

Умереть со скуки<>

Meaning: Something is so dull and tedious that you are beginning to wonder if you will survive the experience.

Example: If I have to sit through one more of Professor Ham's classes, I might die of boredom.

Divide and rule (conquer)

הפרד ומשול<>

Разделяй и властвуй <>

Meaning: The action of separation performed by superior person to subordinates in order to rule them easily.

Example: The elites always like to use the principle of "divide and rule" in order to subjugate the lower classes.

Do a 180

לעשות 180 מעלות (Do a 180 degrees)

Развернутся на 180 градусов (Turn 180 degrees)

Meaning: To completely reverse one's position or opinion on a matter.

Example: I never wanted to get married, but when I met my husband I did a 180 on the subject of marriage!

Domino effect

אפקט הדומינו<>

Эффект домино <>

Meaning: One event can spark a chain reaction, like one domino falling into another, which falls into another, etc.

Example: First Betty's dog chased the cat, which knocked over the punch bowl, which made her scream and wake the baby. It was just a domino effect from that point.

Don't do to others what you don't want others to do to you

אל(Don't do to your friend what you hate by yourself)
תעשה לחברך מה ששנוא עליך

Не делай другим того чего не желаешь себе<>

Meaning: Treat others in the manner that you wish to be treated.

Example: I had to teach Sammy to play nicely with his little sister. I told him "don't do to others what you don't want others to do to you."

Don't kill the messenger

<>אל תהרוג את השליח

Не убивайте вестника, принесшего дурные вести
(Don't kill the messenger bringing the bad news)

Meaning: Do not blame or react angrily to somebody who brings bad news.

Example: Sarah said to John that his son uses drugs, but John did not know the idiom "don't kill the messenger" and began to shout at Sarah.

E

Early bird catches the worm

כל הקודם זוכה(First come rewarded)

Кто рано встаёт тому Бог даёт (God helps those who wake up early)

Meaning: Those who plan ahead and/or arrive early receive the best rewards.

Example: Kenneth is the early bird that got the worm with this promotion. Every day he comes in half an hour earlier than his coworkers.

Easy come easy go

<>בא בקלות הולך בקלות

Пришло махом ушло прахом<>

Meaning: This refers to a nonchalant attitude about things changing, particularly acquiring or losing possessions.

Example: Dotty never worries about money, making it or spending it. Easy come, easy go, that's how Dotty thinks.

Empty words

<>מילים ריקים מתוכן

Пустые слова<>

Meaning: Statements and promises that sound good but have no meaning.

Example: Vivian finally realized Rodolfo's promises to change were just empty words and she left him.

Exception that proves the rule

<>יוצא מן הכלל המעיד על הכלל

Исключение, подтверждающее правило<>

Meaning: A stand-out person or situation that makes it clear that the "rule" or accepted pattern is true.

Example: Matilda is the only one of my four sisters that always does her homework and she gets great grades, the exception that proves the rule.

Eyes are the window to the soul

עיניים ראי לנפש<>

Глаза - зеркало души<>

Meaning: The eyes convey expression and emotion.

Example: I know Gerard doesn't speak much, but I understand him. His eyes are the window to his soul.

Eye for an eye and a tooth for a tooth

עין תחת עין שן תחת שן<>

Око за око, зуб за зуб <>

Meaning: Whatever crime has been committed or injury has been given, the perpetrator receives the same injury in return.

Example: Xavier was framed for drug possession after he framed a rival gang leader, a clear case of an eye for an eye and a tooth for a tooth.

F

Fair game

משחק הוגן<>

Справедливая игра <>

Meaning: The object that is desired is open to any attempts to achieve it or possess it.

Example: Marla announced that she has broken off her engagement, making her fair game to date again.

Fight tooth and nail

נלחם בשיניים(Fight tooth)

Бороться изо всех сил (Fight by all means)

Meaning: To fight with as much force and power as you can muster.

Example: Linda escaped her attackers, fighting them off tooth and nail until she could run away.

Find a place in the sun

למצוא מקום תחת השמש (Find place under the sun)

Найти место под солнцем (Find place under the sun)

Meaning: Find a situation or a mindset that makes you feel confident and happy.

Example: I know it's a rough time right now, but once you find your place in the sun everything will seem much better.

Fingers crossed

להחזיק אצבעות (Hold the fingers)

Постучать по дереву (Knock the wood)

Meaning: A wish based on a superstitious sign for good luck.

Example: We are keeping our fingers crossed for Julia's audition to be successful.

Flesh and blood

בשר ודם<>

Кровь и плоть <>

Meaning: This refers to being biologically related or the husband/wife relationship.

Example: It was hard to believe that John's son was his own flesh and blood since they acted nothing alike.

Food for thought

חומר למחשבה (Stuff for thought)

Пища для размышления<>

Meaning: A subject for deep mental contemplation or consideration.

Example: The book certainly provided some food for thought on the matter of adoption.

Forbidden fruit

פרי אסור<>

Запретный плод<>

Meaning: This refers to something that is desired but inaccessible or not allowed, usually for moral reasons.

Example: Jenna is attracted to her boss, but she knows that he is forbidden fruit.

Friend in need is a friend in deed

חבר בשעת צרה (Friend in a time of trouble)

Друг познаётся в беде (A friend is known due to trouble)

Meaning: A true friend will prove their love through actions and deeds when you need them, not simply claim to be your friend.

Example: Robert proved a friend in need is a friend in deed when he showed up to help us repair our house after the storm.

G

Getting up on the wrong side of the bed

לקום ברגל שמאל (Getting up on the left leg)

Встать с левой ноги (Getting up on the left leg)

Meaning: A person who wakes up in the morning already in a bad mood, for no apparent reason.

Example: Carla is being such a grouch today. I guess she must have gotten up on the wrong side of the bed.

Give a chance

<>לתת צ'אנס

Дать шанс<>

Meaning: Allow someone to have an opportunity.

Example: Diana is so upset that no one gave her a chance to explain what really happened at the party.

Give him an inch and he'll take a mile

(Give him a finger and he wants the whole hand)

נותנים לו אצבע והוא רוצה את כל היד

Дай ему палец он и всю руку откусит (Give him a finger and he will bite off the whole hand)

Meaning: Someone offered a small amount takes much more than they were offered

Example: Don't invite Florian to stay overnight, he'll be here a month! You know him, give him an inch and he'll take a mile.

Give tacit approval

הסכמה בשתיקה (Silent agreement)

Дать молчаливое согласие<>

Meaning: To appear to agree though no explicit statement of agreement was made.

Example: Julian didn't say yes, but he hasn't made any objections. Let's go ahead with the plan and say we have his tacit approval.

Give the green light

<>לתת אור ירוק

Давать зелёный свет<>

Meaning: You are free to proceed or start.

Example: Gregory talked to the school board and they gave him the green light to hire another teacher.

Glass ceiling

<>תקרת זכוכית

Стеклянный потолок<>

Meaning: A metaphor for a difficult top barrier that is hard to breach, especially in the business world.

Example: Berneata became the first woman to break the glass ceiling in her firm's history and become CEO.

Go against the grain

לשחות נגד הזרם (Swim against the flow)

Плыть против течения (Swim against the flow)

Meaning: To go against the accepted opinion of the majority.

Example: John, who had unpopular political views, went against the grain and won the elections.

Go in circles

<>ללכת מסביב

Ходить кругами <>

Meaning: To go over the same material repeatedly without ever making a decision or reaching a conclusion.

Example: I know it's a complex issue, but we have been going in circles for hours, we need to make a decision.

Go for broke

ללכת על כל הקופה(Go for the jackpot)

Идти ва банк (Go for the bank)

Meaning: Giving your utmost to accomplish something you believe in or want to achieve.

Example: No one believed the horse could win, but his trainer went for broke and entered him anyway.

Go from bad to worse

<>הולך מדחי לדחי

Становится всё хуже и хуже (Become worse and worse)

Meaning: The situation is deteriorating instead of improving.

Example: Well, first Margaret had a cold, but then it turned into bronchitis, and now her husband has it too. Things are going from bad to worse in their home.

Good Samaritan

שומרוני הטוב<>

Добрый Самаритянин<>

Meaning: This refers to the Biblical story of the Samaritan who went out of his way to help and care for a wounded stranger. A good Samaritan provides help without expecting anything in return, even to someone he does not know.

Example: The drowning boy was pulled from the lake by a good Samaritan passing by.

Go too far

ללכת רחוק מדי<>

Зайти слишком далеко <>

Meaning: You have overstepped boundaries or pushed the limits.

Example: I didn't mind when Sammy brought home a second cat, but today he brought home three more! He's gone too far this time!

Go with the flow

לשחות עם הזרם)(To swim with the flow)

Плыть по течению <>

Meaning: Move with the situation and not fight against events.

Example: The relocation was unexpected, but Melanie just smiled and said she would go with the flow.

God helps those who help themselves

<>אלוהים עוזר למי שעוזר לעצמו

Бог помогает тому кто помогает себе<>

Meaning: Those who try to do something to better their situation will be blessed by God as well. Do not expect a favor from higher powers if you are unwilling to take action yourself.

Example: Stop sitting and moping about all the damage to the house. You need to start fixing things. After all, God helps those who help themselves.

Grass is always greener on the other side of the fence

הדשא של השכן ירוק יותר (Neighbors grass is greener)

У соседа трава зеленее (Neighbors grass is greener)

Meaning: Someone else's situations or possessions always seem more favorable than your own.

Example: Harvey never seems to be content as long as his friends have something he doesn't. Some day he will learn the grass isn't always greener on the other side of the fence.

Green with envy

ירוק מקנאה<>

Зеленый от зависти<>

Meaning: To be sick with jealousy or longing for something that belongs to someone else.

Example: When Merle saw Bella's dress, she was positively green with envy.

H

Habit is second nature

הרגל הופך לטבע(Habit becomes nature)

Привычка - вторая натура<>

Meaning: A routine or repeated action can soon become instinctive.

Example: My father was furious when he found out my brother started smoking and warned him that habit is second nature.

Hands are tied

ידיים כבולות<>

Руки связаны<>

Meaning: You are unable to take any action.

Example: I really wish I could help, but my hands are tied.

Happy medium

לבחור את שביל הזהב (Choose the golden path)

Выбрать золотую середину <>

Meaning: Choosing the compromise between two extreme options.

Example: I prefer not to vote for far right and far left politicians, but to choose the happy medium.

Hard nut (to crack)

<>אגוז קשה

Крепкий орешек <>

Meaning: A very difficult and stubborn person.

Example: Jane can be kind, but she seems grumpy. She's just a hard nut to crack.

Haste makes waste

החיפזון מהשטן (Haste from a devil)

Поспешишь — людей насмешишь (Haste makes people laugh)

Meaning: Rushing to complete something often means you end up doing more damage and creating more expense.

Example: Ruth tried to repaint the living room in one afternoon. It looked so bad that she had to hire professional painters to fix it. Haste makes waste, and she found out the hard way.

Have a sixth sense

החוש השישי (Sixth sense)

Иметь шестое чувство<>

Meaning: An uncanny ability to sense or know things, often considered a bit psychic or mystical.

Example: Charlie never loses at the track; he has a sixth sense about picking winners.

Have no backbone

חסר חוט שדרה<>

Бесхребетный <>

Meaning: This means a person is weak and has no strong character. They can be easily swayed or persuaded, even against their own best interests.

Example: Marianne knew it was a risk to her frail health, but she let Keith talk her into riding the roller coaster. She has no backbone when it comes to standing up for herself.

Have the last word

להגיד מילה אחרונה (Say the last word)

Сказать последнее слово (Say the last word)

Meaning: Having the final say in an argument.

Example: It is a waste of time to keep talking to Jack; he always has to have the last word.

He who laughs last, laughs best

<>צוחק מי שצוחק אחרון

Смеётся тот кто смеёеся последним <>

Meaning: Being happy and successful in the end is what really matters

Example: Daniel started out poor and unpopular, but now he is a millionaire with a beautiful family. He has laughed last, and laughed best.

He has a thick skin

יש לו עור של פיל (He has a skin of elephant)

Толстокожий<>

Meaning: A person is not easily offended or upset if they have a thick skin.

Example: Gus knew he needed to develop a thick skin if he wanted to work on the police force.

Heart of gold

<>לב של זהב

Золотое сердце<>

Meaning: A person with a heart of gold has a genuinely sweet, kind, and giving nature.

Example: Maude might be a bit disorganized, but she is loved for her giving nature and her heart of gold.

History repeats itself

<>היסטוריה חוזרת על עצמה

История повторяется<>

Meaning: Events will repeat themselves as situations that happened long ago can happen again in different contexts.

Example: Nolan felt like history was repeating itself when he watched his second wife pack her bags and leave.

How time flies

איך הזמן עובר (How time passes)

Как бежит время (How time runs)

Meaning: The time seems to pass very quickly when a person does not realize that time is passing.

Example: I couldn't believe it when the band stopped playing at midnight. I felt like I had just started dancing even though the party started hours ago. How time flies!

I

I am out of words

אין לי מילים<>

У меня нет слов<>

Meaning: There is nothing left to be said on the matter.

Example: I can't believe my cousin is going to marry that scoundrel. I am simply out of words.

It is no use crying over spilt milk

לא בוכים על חלב שנשפך (Do not cry over spilt milk)

О пролитом молоке не плачут (About spilt milk do not cry)

Meaning: What has happened has happened and cannot be undone, so it is pointless to grieve

Example: June was sobbing because she tore her skirt. Michael told her to cheer up and not to cry over spilled milk.

It is not the end of the world

<>זה לא סוף העולם

Это не конец света<>

Meaning: A situation is not as dire as it seems.

Example: I know you lost your job, but you will find another one soon. It's not the end of the world.

It goes in one ear and out the other

<>נכנס מאוזן אחד ויוצא מהשנייה

В одно ухо входит а из другого выходит<>

Meaning: A person hears what you say, but does not remember it or pay attention to it.

Example: No one brought in the assignment as directed. The teacher's instructions went in one ear and out the other.

It takes two to tango

צריכים שניים לטנגו (Need two for tango)

Для танго нужны двое (Need two for tango)

Meaning: A certain relationship cannot be one sided; two people must be involved.

Example: Maria, stop blaming everything on Mandy and admit your part in the fight. You know it takes two to tango.

Ivory tower

<>מגדל שן

Башня из слоновой кости <>

Meaning: If someone is said to be in an ivory tower, it means they have distanced themselves from reality or the world around them, or they think they are above the rest of the world and deserve special treatment.

Example: Wilma mentally lives in her ivory tower and refuses to acknowledge that her neighborhood is going through difficult times.

J

Jump on the bandwagon

<>לקפוץ על עגלה

Запрыгнуть в последний вагон<>

Meaning: Join a cause or movement because everyone else is doing the same.

Example: Horace jumped on the presidential bandwagon to fit in, not because he really enjoys politics.

Jump through hoops

לעשות שמיניות באוויר (Do figure-eights in the air)

Прыгнуть выше головы (Jump beyond the head)

Meaning: This refers to going through many obstacles in order to complete a task or please someone.

Example: I quit my job because I was tired of jumping through hoops to do simple assignments for my demanding boss.

Just in the nick of time

בדקה התשעים (On the ninetieth minute)

В последнию минуту (In the last moment)

Meaning: To complete something at the last moment or before a disaster occurs.

Example: The phone call from the governor came just in the nick of time in order to stop the prisoner's execution.

K

Keep a low profile

>>שמור על פרופיל נמוך

Не привлекать к себе внимания (Do not draw attention for yourself)

Meaning: This indicates a person does not share much information and wants to stay unnoticed, and is often secretive and/or reclusive.

Example: Luke keeps a low profile since retiring from the FBI.

Keep your head above water

>>להחזיק את הראש מעל המיים

Держаться наплаву <>

Meaning: A state where a person is barely managing to keep themselves from financial or physical ruin.

Example: Hector's business is scraping along. He is barely keeping his head above water these days.

Kill two birds with one stone

להרוג שני ציפורים במכה אחת (Kill two birds in one blow)

Убить одним выстрелом двух зайцев (Kill two hares with one shot)

Meaning: This refers to accomplishing two goals through one action or at the same time.

Example: Why don't we stop and visit Uncle Ricky on the way to the beach and kill two birds with one stone?

Kill the goose that lays the golden eggs

להרוג תרנגולת שמטילה ביצי זהב (Kill the hen that lays the golden eggs)

Убить курицу несущую золотые яйца (Kill the hen that lays the golden eggs)

Meaning: This refers to harming or ruining a beneficial relationship, usually causing a benefactor to stop giving support.

Example: I can't believe Sonny would pick a fight with the dean while his scholarship is on the line! Talk about killing the goose that lays the golden eggs!

Kindred spirit

נפש תאומה (Soul twin)

Родная душа <>

Meaning: Someone who has the same passions and opinions as you, creating a harmonious friendship.

Example: Philip and Mary come from such different backgrounds, but they are very much kindred spirits.

Knifing someone in the back

<>תקע לו סכין בגב

Вонзил нож в сердце (Knifing someone in the heart)

Meaning: Being betrayed by someone you trusted.

Example: After working together for fifteen years, I caught Ethel embezzling from our joint account! I can't believe she would stab me in the back like that!

Knock on wood

<>לדפוק על העץ

Постучать по дереву <>

Meaning: A reference to a superstition that knocking on wood will keep a bad event from happening or ensure a good event will occur.

Example: Well, Joe is out of his cast and should be off crutches in a week, knock on wood.

L

Last but not least

אחרון חביב (The last is nice)

Хоть и последний но не менее важный<>

Meaning: The last person/item mentioned, usually in a list, is not the least valuable.

Example: I'd like to thank Tom, Dick, Harry, and last, but not least, Benny, for their fabulous performances tonight.

Light at the end of the tunnel

<>אור בקצה המנהרה

Свет в конце тоннеля<>

Meaning: When going through a bleak or dark time emotionally or mentally, this expression is used to encourage that there is hope, or that there is something positive about to happen.

Example: After six months of chemo, the blood tests are starting to show improvement. Dad now says he sees a light at the end of the tunnel.

Like looking for a needle in a haystack

<>לחפש מחט בערימת שחת

Искать иголку в стоге сена <>

Meaning: Looking for something that is well hidden, or is easily overlooked because of its surroundings.

Example: I can't believe you lost the green hat out here in this huge grassy field. I'll help you find it, but it will be like looking for a needle in a haystack.

Look a gift horse in the mouth

סוס שניתן (Do not check the teeth of a gift horse) במתנה אין בודקים בשיניו

Дареному коню в зубы не смотрят (Do not look the teeth of a gift horse)

Meaning: Looking critically at a gift instead of accepting it with thanks. It can also refer to anyone being critical of a windfall or helpful act.

Example: Jake doesn't enjoy Penny's company but since she offered to help repair the fence, I told him not to look a gift horse in the mouth.

M

Make a mountain out of a molehill

לעשות פיל מזבוב (Make a fly out of elephant)

Сделать из мухи слона (Make a fly out of elephant)

Meaning: A small matter has been exaggerated until it becomes a giant problem.

Example: Carrie lost her car in the parking lot at a mall, but she made a mountain out of a molehill. Before long, she had security and police searching for a car thief.

Money doesn't grow on trees

<>כסף לא גדל על העצים

Деньги не растут на деревьях <>

Meaning: Money is earned by hard work; it is not something that naturally occurs, or replenishes itself. It is typically a reminder to spend carefully.

Example: Your father is never going to be able to afford all these dresses! Don't you realize that money doesn't grow on trees?

Much ado about nothing

<>הרבה מהומה על לא מאומה

Много шума из ничего <>

Meaning: To give a trivial incident huge importance.

Example: "I heard a bike was stolen in the neighborhood. Police are investigating."

"I bet some kid borrowed it, just a case of much ado about nothing."

Murphy's Law

<>חוק מרפי

Закон Мерфи<>

Meaning: The belief that if something can go wrong, it will go wrong.

Example: Earnest knew that if something could go wrong on his wedding day, it probably would. He had a healthy respect for Murphy's Law.

N

Need something like a hole in the head

<צריך את זה כמו חור בראש>

Нужно как зайцу стоп-сигнал (Need like a stop sign for a hare)

Meaning: Something that is clearly bad or unwanted.

Example: Pablo's mother-in-law and her six elderly cats are moving in with him. Boy, he needs that like a hole in the head.

Neither fish nor fowl

<פרווה>

Ни рыба ни мясо<>

Meaning: Someone or something having a character that is hard to define.

Example: I've been trying to get to know Mr. Yin, but he seems very enigmatic. It's a case of neither fish nor fowl every time we talk.

New broom sweeps clean

מטאטא חדש מטאטא טוב<>

Новая метла метёт по новому <>

Meaning: A fresh/new leader in charge makes many "clean sweeps", drastic changes.

Example: Doreen is afraid her department will change a lot with the new boss arriving. He has a bit of a "new broom sweeps clean" reputation.

Nip it in the bud

לגדוע באיבו<>

Уничтожить в зародыше <>

Meaning: To end something before it develops, referring to removing the bud before a plant can flower.

Example: Gina went on a date with some thug, but just once. Her father nipped that in the bud right away.

No such animal

<>אין חיה כזאת

Нет такого животного<>

Meaning: Something is too unlikely or impossible to believe.

Example: You are telling me that the swindler is really giving all his profits to a tiny orphanage you've never heard of? Sorry, there's no such animal.

No smoke without fire

<>אין עשן בלי אש

Нет дыма без огня <>

Meaning: There is no appearance or indicator of wrongdoing without some actual wrongdoing occurring.

Example: Some people say that there was nothing suspicious about Mrs. Smith leaving Mr. Jones' house in the middle of the night, but I say there is no smoke without fire.

Nothing new under the sun

<>שום דבר חדש מתחת לשמש

Ничего нового под солнцем <>

Meaning: Something may seem new, but in reality it is just a variation of something that already has existed or happened.

Example: The genocide in the Middle East is shocking, but sadly, it's nothing new under the sun.

O

On cloud nine

בשמיים(In the sky)

На седьмом небе (On the seventh sky)

Meaning: A state of intense happiness and joy.

Example: Ellen just accepted my proposal! I'm on cloud nine!

Once in a blue moon

פעם ביובל (Once in a fifty years)

Раз в сто лет (Once in a hundred years)

Meaning: A rare occurrence, something that hardly ever happens.

Example: The hermit comes down to the village once in a blue moon, but he never stays long.

One hand washes the other

יד רוחצת יד<>

Рука руку моет<>

Meaning: A partnership or collusion, usually something sneaky or underhanded, where one favor is given in exchange for another

Example: Rory repairs the cars that Vito vandalized and gives him a percentage of the money he makes. One hand washes the other, but soon they will both be caught!

Open Pandora's Box

לפתוח תיבת פנדורה<>

Открыть ящик Пандоррры<>

Meaning: In Greek mythology Pandora's Box was the box that contained all the evils of humanity. When it was opened, all of the evils escaped and began to plague earth. Figuratively, when someone opens Pandora's Box, it means that they have unleashed an unpleasant or bad situation or series of events.

Example: Bringing up Rose's previous relationships in front of her new husband really opened up Pandora's Box.

Out of the blue

לפתע פתאום (All of a sudden)

Как гром среди ясного неба (As thunder out of the blue sky)

Meaning: Something comes as a complete shock and is utterly unexpected.

Example: It was completely out of the blue when Aidan declared he was leaving home.

Over my dead body

<>על גופתי המתה

Через мой труп <>

Meaning: This expression indicates extremely strong objections, and that the person will only allow the event to happen after they have died and can no longer raise objections. This expression indicates that a person will do everything in their power to stop whatever they are objecting to from occurring.

Example: If you want to drop out of school, you will do it over my dead body!

P

Play cat and mouse

<>משחק חתול ועכבר

Игра в кошки-мышки<>

Meaning: To engage in a back-and-forth argument or exchange.

Example: I wish Doris and Flo would stop this stupid cat-and-mouse war they have on Facebook.

Pull strings

<>למשוך בחוטים

Дёргать за ниточки<>

Meaning: Using influence or connections to get something that you want that would otherwise be unavailable.

Example: I know the concert is sold out, but I have a friend in the ticket office who is going to pull some strings for me so I can go.

Pull one's chestnuts out of the fire

<>להוציא ערמונים מהאש

Таскать каштаны из огня<>

Meaning: To get out of a dangerous or detrimental situation at the last minute.

Example: With just ten minutes left to register for the spring semester at college, Terrence managed to contact the registrar. He pulled his chestnuts out of the fire.

Push at an open door

התפרץ לדלת פתוחה (Break into an open door)

Ломиться в открытую дверь (Break into an open door)

Meaning: Working at something that is already happening, or is going to happen easily.

Example: John tried to convince his boss to begin a new project. The manager said, "I am already convinced and you are pushing at an open door."

Put the cart before the horse

<<לשים עגלה לפני הסוסים

Делать что-либо "шиворот-навыворот" (Do something topsy-turvy)

Meaning: Acting prematurely, or doing things out of the most logical order.

Example: I told Vick that carpeting before painting was putting the cart before the horse, but he wouldn't listen.

Put a spoke in the wheel (Put a monkey wrench in the works)

<<לשים מקלות בגלגלים

Вставлять палки в колёса<>

Meaning: To spoil someone's plans or stop a project.

Example: I can't believe Frankie put a spoke in the wheel when we were so close to finishing our group presentation.

Put something on the back burner

על אש הקטנה (On the back burner)

На медленном огне (On the back burner)

Meaning: A matter is not going to be the primary focus right now; it will receive delayed attention.

Example: The school board discussed the budget and decided that the new soccer field could be put on the back burner.

R

Rat race

<>מרוץ עכברים

Крысиные бега<>

Meaning: A high-pressure, stressful environment from which one feels like they cannot escape.

Example: Working in London but living in the suburbs gives me a bit of a break from the rat race.

Ray of hope

<>קרן תקווה

Луч надежды<>

Meaning: Even in a dark situation, there is a glimmer of positivity.

Example: Though the circumstances looked grim, one ray of hope was that the family became closer.

Read between the lines

<>לקרוא בין השורות

Читать между строк<>

Meaning: Able to infer meaning or information that isn't explicitly stated.

Example: No one told Shane that he wasn't welcome, but he could read between the lines.

Roll up one's sleeves

<>להפשיל שרוולים

Засучить рукава<>

Meaning: Preparing for intense labor or effort.

Example: There is so much to be done before the family comes to stay for the week. We'd better roll up our sleeves and get to work.

Rub salt into the wound

לזרוח מלח על הפצעים<>

Сыпать соль на раны <>

Meaning: Salt in an open wound increases pain and adds burning and stinging. Rubbing salt in the wound figuratively means to add additional pain when someone is already hurt or upset.

Example: Bonnie was in tears when she lost the beauty contest, but when her sister won, it was rubbing salt in the wound.

S

Sacred cow

<>פרה קדושה

Священная корова <>

Meaning: An object is held in reverence.

Example: Grandma Maher's locket has been passed down for ten generations and has become something of a sacred cow to the women of the family.

Salt of the earth

<>מלח הארץ

Соль земли<>

Meaning: To be an honest and uncomplicated person who is well thought of.

Example: You can trust William to help anyone in need; he's salt of the earth and a great guy.

Save for a rainy day

<>לחסוך ליום סגריר

Сохранить на черный день (Save for a black day)

Meaning: To put something aside for the future, especially a difficult or lean time where you may need to draw on savings or stockpile.

Example: I always put five percent of my paycheck away for a rainy day.

See eye to eye

<>לראות עין בעין

Сходится во взглядах <>

Meaning: To have the same viewpoint, to be in agreement on an issue.

Example: Jorge and I argue a lot, but we always see eye to eye when it comes to politics.

See which way the wind is blowing

<>ראה לאן נושבת הרוח

Смотреть куда ветер дует<>

Meaning: To observe which way a trend is going, or which direction a topic is heading.

Example: Mona won't tell anyone her opinion of the candidates too early. She says she likes to do her research, but I think she just wants to see which way the wind is blowing.

Separate the wheat from the chaff

(Distinguish between the central aspect and the להבדיל בין עיקר לתפל unimportant)

Отделять зерна от плевел<>

Meaning: Separating good and bad individuals, items, or can refer to separating quality from inferior items.

Example: The headmaster looked at the group he would divide into advances and regular classes and said, "It's time to separate the wheat from the chaff."

Silence is golden

<<שתיקה שווה זהב>

Молчание – золото <>

Meaning: In this case silence is highly prized and desired.

Example: Ask any mother with a fussy baby and she will tell you that silence is golden.

Sisyphean task

<>עבודה סיזיפית>

Сизифов труд <>

Meaning: Unpleasant, never-ending chore or effort.

Example: With seven people in our family, the laundry has become a Sisyphean task.

Sky is the limit

<>שמיים הם הגבול

Небо - это предел<>

Meaning: There is no limit to how much you can achieve or advance.

Example: Dawn began to doubt herself, but her coach told her the sky was the limit and she persevered.

Slim to none

<>שואף לאפס

Стремится к нулю<>

Meaning: There is almost no chance of something happening.

Example: The forecast says that the chance of precipitation is slim to none.

Smoke like a chimney

<>מעשן כמו קטר

Дымит как паравоз (Smoke like locomotive)

Meaning: To obsessively smoke cigarettes, creating the impression that you produce as much smoke as a fire puts out of a chimney.

Example: I am so mad that my mother-in-law still smokes like a chimney, even though she knows her son has asthma.

Stay afloat

<>לצוף על פני המים

Оставаться на плаву <>

Meaning: Managing to survive or keep going, but just barely.

Example: The cafe has fewer customers since the new restaurant opened across the street. I don't think they can stay afloat much longer

Steal the show

<>גנב את ההצגה

Переключить внимание на себя (Switch attention to yourself)

Meaning: To outperform someone.

Example: Candace is such a brilliant scientist that she stole the show from her professor in class.

Straw that broke the camel's back

<>הקש ששבר את גב הגמל

Соломинка переломившая спину верблюду<>

Meaning: This is the final burden or stimulus that causes someone or something to fail or lose control.

Example: Danielle stayed calm when the cab driver showed up late. She was okay when she lost one of her suitcases at the airport. The straw that broke the camel's back was finding out that her flight was delayed by three hours.

Strike while the iron is hot

<>להכות בברזל בעודו חם

Куй железо пока горячо<>

Meaning: Acting at the right moment; acting quickly to get a great opportunity.

Example: They are giving free trips to Disneyland if you call in the next ten minutes! Hurry and get to the phone, strike while the iron is hot!

T

Take the bull by the horns

<>אאחז את השור בקרניו

Взять быка за рога<>

Meaning: Confront the problem directly.

Example: Beth thought she saw her student cheating on his math test, but she was reluctant to take the bull by the horns and ask him about it.

Take it into his head

<>הכניס לעצמו לראש

Взял себе в голову <>

Meaning: To have the idea or notion come to mind.

Example: Walter was afraid that reading so many mysteries would make his son take it into his head to start his own detective agency.

Take the law into your own hands

<>לוקח את החוק בידיים

Взял закон в свои руки <>

Meaning: When regular citizens try to get justice themselves, outside of the legal system, instead of waiting for the police or lawyers to intervene when an injustice occurs.

Example: Ronan saw the man who mugged his wife walking down the street. He took the law into his own hands and tackled the man to the pavement.

Talk somebody's head off

לבלבל את המח (Mess the mind)

Морочить голову (Mess the mind)

Meaning: To be extremely talkative, to the point where the listener feels like they are going crazy or are completely frustrated.

Example: Edna lives all alone and is quite lonesome. When she has company, she will talk someone's head off.

The best defense is a good offense

<>ההגנה הכי טובה היא התקפה

Лучшая оборона - это нападение<>

Meaning: Making a strong first movement is better preparation for a battle than waiting to defend once you are attacked.

Example: Mr. Bollinger's lawyer had a beautiful opening statement, and left the jury applauding. He knows that the best defense is a good offense.

The best is the enemy of the good

<>האויב של הטוב הוא המצוין

Лучшее враг хорошего<>

Meaning: Attributed to a French philosopher Voltaire, this idiom means that perfection is the preferred state of being; good pales in comparison to the best.

Example: The 1998 Bordeaux was very nice, but the 1993 was outstanding! We definitely want a case of the '93, after all the best is the enemy of the good.

The customer is always right

<>לקוח תמיד צודק

Клиент всегда прав<>

Meaning: In order to promote the best service, many businesses adopted the motto that the customer was always right, meaning that whatever the customer wanted, it needed to be delivered.

Example: Mrs. Sondberg made strange requests, but the manager says the customer is always right.

The end justifies the means

<>המטרה מקדשת את האמצעים

Цель оправдывает средства<>

Meaning: Whatever actions are needed to complete the goal are allowable, even if they are somewhat unethical or illegal actions.

Example: Jody forged his mother's signature in order to check himself into rehab, figuring the end justified the means.

The fish always stinks from the head

<>הדג מסריח מהראש

Рыба гниёт с головы (The fish rots from the head)

Meaning: If an organization or operation is found to be corrupt, it is probable that the leaders are involved, not just the underlings in the company.

Example: The CEO, Mr. Nagi, was found guilty of fraud. The police always believed this was a case of the fish stinking from the head.

The fifth column

<>גייס החמישי

Пятая колонна<>

Meaning: A group of people who work to destroy a larger group from within.

Example: Radical forces started a raid in the city. By dawn, the fifth column's actions had created immense destruction.

The last bastion

מעוז אחרון<>

Последний оплот<>

Meaning: A final or only remaining element of its kind.

Example: The mind is the last bastion of free speech in these troubled times.

The left hand doesn't know what the right hand is doing

יד ימין לא יודעת מיד שמאל<>

Правая рука не знает, что делает левая<>

Meaning: This indicates confusion and disorder (or in some cases dishonesty) within a single organization or system.

Example: Accounting said my papers were in billing, but billing said the papers were in the mail, proving the left hand didn't know what the right hand was doing

The moment of truth

<>רגע האמת

Момент истины<>

Meaning: A time when all is revealed, nothing is hidden. Everyone can see what is true.

Example: Evelyn has been attending culinary school for a year. Tonight is the moment of truth; she is cooking for her father.

The road to hell is paved with good intentions

<>הדרך לגיהנום רצופה כוונות טובות

Дорога в ад вымощена благими намерениями<>

Meaning: Good intentions, as opposed to good deeds. In order for good things to be done, you cannot just intend to do something, you must take action.

Example: Tiana is always saying she will go out and volunteer, or get up early and exercise, but all she does is play games on her computer. I wonder if she knows that the road to hell is paved with good intentions.

The sword of Damocles

<>חרב דמוקלס

Дамоклов меч<>

Meaning: In reference to a Greek myth, this is a term meaning that those in power are always in danger or under threat.

Example: Mr. Baker is just a humble clerk, but he is certain he is always under the sword of Damocles.

The tail wagging the dog

<>הזנב מכשכש בכלב

Хвост виляет собакой<>

Meaning: Somebody who is supposed to be under supervision controls the situation

Example: Everyone knew the changes in the company were caused by the tail wagging the dog, and the tail was Lorelei, the managing director's mistress.

The walls have ears

יש אוזניים לכותל<>

Стены имеют уши <>

Meaning: This refers to people eavesdropping and spying. You have to be cautious of what you say and where you say it, because you could be overheard and reported.

Example: Darla told Steven they could not talk until after they left the mansion. "I have an uneasy feeling that the walls have ears in that place," she proclaimed.

There is no accounting for tastes

על טעם וריח (Do not argue about a taste and smell) אין להתווכח

О вкусах не спорят (Do not argue about a taste)

Meaning: All individuals have different likes and dislikes. We cannot figure out why some people enjoy things and others don't.

Example: Ursula hates jazz, but Miles loves it. Oh well, there's no accounting for tastes, is there?

There is no such thing as a free lunch

אין ארוחות חינם<>

Бесплатных обедов не бывает<>

Meaning: Everything has a price, financial or otherwise.

Example: Barbara was shocked when her date said he expected her to come home with him after their dinner, but apparently he believed there was no such thing as a free lunch.

Think outside the box

לחשוב מחוץ לקופסה<>

Думать неординарно (Think extraordinary)

Meaning: To think or behave in an unexpected and creative manner.

Example: I know we can find a solution to the problem if we start thinking outside the box.

Throw down the glove

<>לזרוק את הכפפה

Бросать вызов (To throw a challenge)

Meaning: Derived from dueling, throwing down the glove means that somebody is offering a challenge or confrontation.

Example: Amos regretted throwing down the glove at the tennis courts once he learned that Hannah was a champion tennis player in the top seed.

Throw out the baby with the bathwater

<>לשפוך את התינוק עם המים

Выплеснуть ребенка вместе с водой<>

Meaning: Do not accidentally get rid of something valuable in the midst of disposing of what is unneeded; and do not lose sight of what is important.

Example: We are cleaning out the attic carefully. I'm glad we didn't decide to throw out everything without sorting. If we had thrown the baby out with the bathwater, we might have gotten rid of some valuable antiques.

Tighten belts

<>להדק חגורות

Затянуть ремни <>

Meaning: Increase frugality and try to make do with less.

Example: Since mother lost her job, we all had to tighten our belts to help with the finances

Time heals everything

<>הזמן מרפא הכל

Время всё лечит<>

Meaning: Even the most horrible pains will fade if given enough time.

Example: Aaron vowed that he would never get over the broken heart his college sweetheart gave him, but time heals everything.

Time is money

<>זמן זה כסף

Время-деньги <>

Meaning: Time is valuable, and even though it does not have a direct monetary value, it is paid for in some fashion.

Example: Please hurry and finish the printing job! We are waiting for the posters to start our campaign, and time is money.

To err is human

<>לטעות זה אנושי

Человеку свойственно ошибаться<>

Meaning: This means that every human is imperfect and will make mistakes.

Example: It does no good to get angry at the children when they make mistakes, for to err is human.

Tomorrow is another day

מחר יום חדש (Tomorrow is a new day)

Даст Бог день даст Бог пищу (God gives you this day, God gives you food)

Meaning: This is an expression meant to give hope, as in there will be another opportunity tomorrow if today was not a success.

Example: Leah looked around at her ruined cake and the terribly messy kitchen and sighed. "Oh well, tomorrow is another day," she told herself.

Turn the other cheek

>להגיש את הלחי השניה<

Подставить другую щеку<>

Meaning: This expression means to show forgiveness, even if someone has injured you.

Example: Joshua knew that George was hurt and angry when he insulted him. Joshua just turned the other cheek and tried to get his friend to calm down.

Turn a blind eye

לעצום עינים (Close eyes)

Закрыть глаза (Close eyes)

Meaning: Ignoring a problem that is obvious.

Example: Jenny's mother turned a blind eye to her father's abuse until the school officials called protective services.

Turn the clock back

<>להחזיר את השעון אחורנית

Повернуть время вспять <>

Meaning: This is a wish to be able to regain time, or make up lost time.

Example: Sally and Henry reunited after twenty years, but both wish they could turn the clock back.

Two sides of the same coin

שני צדדים למטבע<>

Две стороны одной медали<>

Meaning: Two things may seem very different, but yet have more similarities than you would think.

Example: Donna and Celia argue so much, but to anyone who knows them well, they are really two sides of the same coin.

Two heads are better than one

טובים השניים מן האחד (Two are better than one)

Одна голова хорошо, а две лучше<>

Meaning: Two minds can solve a problem better than one; two people working together is more efficient than one.

Example: I am so glad Maurice came over to help with the budget. Two heads are better than one when it comes to math.

U

Upper hand

<>ידו על העליונה

Брать верх (Overpower)

Meaning: To have the advantage over someone else in a situation.

Example: With fifteen years of training, Peter definitely has the upper hand over the other candidates in the interview process.

V

Vicious circle

<>מעגל קסמים

Замкнутый круг (Closed circle)

Meaning: A series of events that connect in a negative and repetitive way.

Example: Every time the dog barks, it makes the baby cry, and every time the baby cries, the dog barks. We were trapped in a vicious circle until the dog went outside.

Vote with one's feet

<>להצביע ברגליים

Голосовать ногами<>

Meaning: To indicate where you stand by your absence.

Example: No one showed up for the mayor's rally. I guess it will be a case of voting with one's feet this election.

W

Wait with bated breath

<>לחכות בקוצר רוח

Ждать с нетерпением (Wait fervently)

Meaning: To wait anxiously and expectantly.

Example: Sarah saw Michael drop to his knee and waited with bated breath for him to propose.

Window of opportunity

<>חלון הזדמנויות

Уникальная возможность (Unique opportunity)

Meaning: A period of opportunity that is brief, or may close at a definite time.

Example: I wish Quentin would hurry up and accept the job offer before he misses the window of opportunity.

Witch hunt

<>ציד מכשפות

Охота на ведьм <>

Meaning: A series of false accusations or time spent looking for fault in order to wrongfully blame someone or convict someone of wrongdoing.

Example: During the vice-principal's annual witch hunt they opened all the student lockers looking for drugs, but didn't find anything

With flying colors

בהצטיינות (With honor)

С триумфом (With triumph)

Meaning: To succeed beyond the standard, with an extremely high degree of excellence.

Example: The Olympic committee said the team passed the qualifier with flying colors.

With friends like that, who needs enemies?

עם חברים כאלה מי צריך אויבים<>

С такими друзьями и враги не нужны<>

Meaning: When someone has relationships with "friends" who do not act as true friends, but rather enemies.

Example: Did you hear what Darcy said about Monica's hair? I thought they were so close, but with friends like that, who needs enemies?

Withstand the test of time

עמד במבחן הזמן<>

Прошел проверку временем <>

Meaning: Something has strength or quality that endures age, injuries, and setbacks.

Example: I know my car is old and battered, but it has withstood the test of time, and I don't want another one.

Wolf in sheep's clothing

<>זאב באור של כבש

Волк в овечьей шкуре <>

Meaning: A person appears to be kind or helpful, but is really looking to injure or take advantage.

Example: Midge seemed kind, but she was a wolf in sheep's clothing who anonymously harassed people.

Would not hurt a fly

<>לא מסוגל לפגוע בזבוב

Мухи не обидит<>

Meaning: A person or animal is so gentle and sweet-natured that they could not do any harm, not even a slight bit.

Example: I know Calvin looks like a big, mean dog, but he's so sweet and he wouldn't hurt a fly!

Y

You are telling me?

<>אתה מספר לי?

Вы мне говорите? <>

Meaning: This indicates shock and disbelief, because the person hearing news is already so clearly aware of it.

Example: "Boy, I guess Fonzie really likes his music loud."

"You're telling me? Remember, he was my roommate for three years!"

Acknowledgments

I am very grateful for my wife Alina, who gave me all possible support for writing this book.

I would like to thank Mary Culler, talented writer and editor who helped me to write the meanings and examples of idioms.

Thanks to my daughter Sarah, who edited the Hebrew idioms.

About the author

Vladimir Marshak, a multilingual certified public accountant, has a wide range of different interests and hobbies like investments, chess, mindfulness etc. But languages are his passion.

For many years Vladimir has been performing language exchange with people from US, Israel, UK, Canada, Australia, New Zeeland and South Africa. Vladimir developed the comprehensive system for deep acquiring foreign languages, in which idiomatic phrases and expressions play a very significant role.

For any questions, language tips and suggestions, please do not hesitate to contact Vladimir Marshak: vmarshak@gmail.com

Made in the USA
Middletown, DE
12 April 2017